GENA'S
POTS AND PANS

How I Built My Village One Bite at a Time

GENA MILLER AND GENEVIEVRE MILLER

Outskirts Press, Inc.
http://www.outskirtspress.com

ISBN: 978-1-9772-2964-9

Cover Photo © 2020 Jamal Miller. All rights reserved - used with permission.
The photographer for the interior images is: Chantale Miller

Outskirts Press and the "OP" logo are trademarks belonging to Outskirts Press, Inc.

PRINTED IN THE UNITED STATES OF AMERICA

HOME

Rue Auxilius Fougere
Les Cayes, Haiti

Table of Contents

Foreword

This is a picture of my grandmother. Her name was Resia Vitale. Make no mistake she's a Queen. She is my Queen. She died when I was 14. She lived in Haiti all her life and was a force to be reckoned with. She didn't know anything about American civil rights and affirmative action, but what I know of her is that she had a powerful presence. She was a woman who believed all women should stand on their own two feet without the support of any man. I love her for instilling incredible work ethics in me, unmatched character, and relentless pursuit of overcoming any obstacles that comes my way.

This is a picture of me and my grandfather. His man named L'herisson Saintervil. To most people he is "boss Didi". To me, this man is God. I will forever be "Ti shoune" to him. (There is no translation, it's just his pet name he used to call me since I was born) He taught me everything I know about life, kindness toward others, independence, and the true meaning of unconditional love. I am so humbly grateful knowing that I share their bloodline.

The Purpose of This Book

Of all things I am most proud of in my life, the village I created is number one. I have been able to make a difference in my world by showing kindness to everyone who have stepped foot into my home.

It starts with the outside entrance of my door with a sign that reads, "Hate has no home here." This couldn't be truer today than in prior years. I have a diverse group of friends from all backgrounds, races, and religions. It's never acceptable to say "small" hateful comments in my presence, regardless how minimal. There's no such thing as "it's just between us," or "I'm only telling you." Absolutely no place for it, and certainly not at my kitchen table.

I single handedly cannot change the world. However, I single handedly have found cooking as my vehicle to make a positive change in the lives of the people who take a bite of my meals.

These recipes are dear to my heart. They require fresh ingredients and lots of love. These recipes cannot be rushed, and as a result, you will be rewarded with an experience you will share with all your family and friends.

Melissa's Tail
(Oxtails)

Melissa is my daughter's roommate from college. They both came home for spring break. Nev knows how much I love having her friends over. Melissa is different from any of her other friends she's brought home before. I liked Melissa from the moment she walked in the door. She had a sweet smile, beautiful face, and kind heart.

It was the last Saturday before COVID-19 was announced. Unbeknownst to all of us, I had no idea it would be the last time for a long time I would be hosting a dinner party for my friends. I had decided to host a housewarming party for our new home. It was going to be a fun night of food, wine, and tons of laughter. Melissa volunteered to help me in the kitchen as my daughters slept. Yes, my children were sleeping as Melissa, the guest in the house, was helping me in the kitchen. Clearly, I did a horrible job as their mother. Melissa and I took this opportunity to bond. We talked like we had been friends forever.

She is such beauty. She asks all sort of interesting questions. For example, have I ever been the only woman of color in a room? Have I ever felt minimized? Do I see hope in the future where racism will not play a part in our daily lives as black women? The answer to all questions were yes especially the latter. For me, I think the racism/sexism is on equal footing. The sexism I continue to experience on a day to day is still profound. I still witness the office "sausage party" (group of men 3 or more gathering to mingle and bond.) Men still get paid more than women. On the racism front, I am often the only black woman in the room. My frustration is perceived as aggressive and abrasive where if it were a man it would be passionate and insightful. What's even more infuriating is when a woman of color points out a problem, it often turns against her as if she is the one who is the problem. You need to be smart to note when it's happening. Hopefully if you do catch it then we have an obligation to check it and hopefully rid it at its onset. It's absolutely frustrating and tiring. These obstacles won't change overnight but like I said, there's progress. For now, let's make those tails ok?

WHAT YOU WILL NEED

For the oxtails
- 2 pounds of oxtails
- 1 cup distilled white vinegar
- 2 teaspoon Adobo seasoning
- 5 fresh garlic cloves
- A handful of fresh cilantro leaves
- 7 bulbs allspice, crushed in the pilón
- ½ a beef bouillon cube
- 1 fresh squeezed lemon
- 2 teaspoons black pepper
- 1 diced fresh tomato
- 2 fresh thyme sprigs
- 1 teaspoon garlic powder
- 1 tablespoon soy sauce
- 1 tablespoon browning Sauce

For the sauce
- 1 tablespoon flour
- 2 teaspoons tomato paste
- Add black pepper
- 1 cup of Fresh cubed onions
- A handful of parsley

PREPARATION

Rinse oxtails with vinegar then rinse with water.

Mix all the remaining ingredients together in a medium size pot.

Let simmer until liquid is evaporated. The fat should render after about 10-15 minutes.

Keep adding ¼ cup of water every 2 minutes until the meat is seared perfectly.

MAKING THE SAUCE

Add tomato paste, a sprinkle of flour, black pepper, onions, parsley and mix vigorously.

Add 4 cups of water until it covers the top of the meat.

Let it simmer on low heat for about 40 minutes.

When sauce thickens, taste and adjust spice as needed.

Serve on a bed of white rice (I suggest my crack rice recipe on the next page).

Crack Rice
(White Rice)

There's funny story behind the name crack rice. It's so simple to cook, and if done correctly people claim it tastes like there's more to it—there must be drugs in this rice. It's impossible that it can taste so good and be so simple to make—it must be crack. Every single person I have served this to can never have enough. I honestly don't understand what the noise is all about, but I must be onto something if everyone—and I mean everyone—insists it's the best white rice they've ever eaten. Here's how you make it. I promise I am not leaving anything out, so give it your best shot.

WHAT YOU WILL NEED

- 3 cups white rice
- 3 cups water
- 2 tablespoons vegetable oil
- 2 tablespoons salt—just plain old salt (not kosher, Himalayan, pink salt etc., none of that)
- 2 teaspoons margarine

PREPARATION

Let water come to a full boil. Add oil.

Wash white rice thoroughly until water is clear. Add rice to 3 cups of boiling water. Stir until rice is grainy, not bulking and sticky. Let it simmer until all water dissipates. Once you can only see rice and not much water, lower heat to its lowest form. Cover rice with a paper towel and use the pan cover to cover for about 15 minutes.

Remove paper towel, add margarine, and fluff with a fork. Recover for 7 minutes.

Turn heat off and let rice sit for 5 minutes before serving.

Lucria's SeaWorld
(Baked Fish)

My oldest daughter Nev earned her degrees in African American studies and Political Science at Pennsylvania State University. A professor at the school is responsible for switching the light on, and man oh man, is the light on. You cannot go an hour with her in the room without a discussion about politics, women, oppression, racism, and suppression. She challenges me to think deeper and she breaks it down like a science. I have always wanted to raise powerful black women—like Oprah Winfrey or Condoleezza Rice. What I got is much more than that. She speaks with passion, certainty, facts, and every now and then will add her opinion. I have no idea how this happened, but it happened, nevertheless.

This behavior was infused by one of our dear friends Lucria. She reminds me a lot of my grandmother. When I am around Lucria, my spirit knows that I am in the presence of greatness. I say this with no exaggeration when I tell you that Lucria is in the same caliber as Michelle Obama—smart, beautiful, gentle, but the worst mistake anyone can make is to underestimate her. One word that describes Lucria: beast.

She's an activist and has been since I met her over fifteen years ago now. If you are fortunate to be in her circle, she gives it to you straight and treats you like family. I remember when she bought her beautiful double-lot house on top of the hill in Teaneck, New Jersey. The house is beautiful. First thing she did was invite me to cook in her gorgeous kitchen. She didn't care what I cooked, but she wanted me to bless her kitchen with one of my Caribbean dishes. More importantly, she wanted me to know that that her home is my home. And if you love cooking, you know if someone allows you to cook in their kitchen that's just an esteemed honor.

One thing I have learned for certain is when Lucria gives you an advice, you take it, run with it, and don't question it. Lucria is the reason Nev wants to pursue law, because Lucria is a lawyer herself. I love to see the two of them together because I watch how Nev looks up to her, really listens to her every word, and mimics her behavior. And when things are going right in my daughter's life, she always asks, "Did you tell Lucria about what I did?"

When Nev is home, we take over the kitchen. This is by far my favorite dish to make with her. It is so delicious. The first bite will require you to close your eyes and give blessings to whichever God you pray to and say "Hallelujah!"

WHAT YOU WILL NEED

- 1 whole fish (about 1 lbs in weight) (I prefer croaker or snapper, head and all. For those of you who are weak, get it fillet. It will taste the same but know that I am laughing at you.)
- Aluminum foil – cut about 12 inches in length
- Shredded cabbage – about 2 cups
- 2 tablespoon of olive oil
- 1 tablespoon of uncooked corn
- 1 sliced okra
- 1 teaspoon of seafood seasoning
- 1 teaspoon Adobo
- 1 sprig of fresh thyme
- A pinch of fresh cilantro leaves
- 2 thin slices of fresh lemon
- 1 pat of salted butter
- 1 teaspoon soy sauce

PREPARATION

Make sure fish is fully cleaned. Wash with lemon juice and then rinse thoroughly.

Place 1 teaspoon of olive oil at the bottom of the foil. Add shredded cabbage. Place fish on top of cabbage.

Add another teaspoon of olive oil on top of fish. Season with Adobo, then add fish seasoning.

Add lemon juice and soy sauce. Place thyme inside and outside of fish. Add corn and okra. Top fish with butter and lemon slices.

Seal the foil. Make sure no air will penetrate the package.

Bake at 350° for 45 minutes, then raise the temperate to 400 for another 15 minutes.

Take it out of the oven and enjoy straight from the foil.

Yeye Cheese Plate
(Mac and Cheese)

I have had the joy of being a part of the upbringing of this beautiful young lady. Her name is Fatou but those who love her call her Yeli, and those who cherish her call her Yeye. I call her Yeye. Her mother, Fatima, is probably the most undiplomatic person I have ever met. When I tell you she tells it like it is, I mean she tells it like it is.

Fatima had to travel on a business trip, and I'll never forget how excited I was when she asked if Yeye could stay with me for a couple of weeks.

I love kids. I love their free spirit, their innocence, and everything about kids that we as adults take for granted. I love Yeye because she exudes all those characteristics, but mostly because she is so wise beyond her years. Academically, I feel she makes all her teachers not just jealous, but I know for a fact they are saying to themselves, "I wish I can be that smart one day." She's funny, witty, and just intellectually superior to anyone I know. During her stay one night, we were driving together while deciding what we were going to have for dinner. I threw a few options at her, but when I said let's go to Panera Bread, her eyes lit up. I followed up by saying, "You like Panera, Yeye?" She replied, "Not really, but I do love their mac and cheese." Naturally, I took it as a challenge and determined to impress her with my mac and cheese.

A week later, I decided to make mac and cheese and all I remember was when she tasted mine she said it wasn't even a competition. I'll never forget her first bite into a plate of my mac and cheese. She placed the fork in her mouth and slowly pulled it out. After the motor of her mouth started churning, she paused and said, "OMG, this is soooooo good." My instant reaction in my mind was, "Bite me, Panera Bread! Yeye chose my mac and cheese over yours. Ha!

WHAT YOU WILL NEED

- 3 cups of 2% milk, warmed
- 2 - 8 oz bag shredded sharp cheese
- 3 teaspoons of butter
- 2 tablespoons flour
- 1 8-oz can of evaporated milk
- 1 lbs of large shells pasta
- 1 tablespoon salt
- 1 tablespoon cracked pepper

PREPARATION

In one hot pan, add the butter until melted. Add flour until it is dissolved. Add the warm milk slowly as you continue to whisk, making sure there are no lumps. Make sure the heat is on low and continue to whisk until the sauce thickens. (Oh yeah, expect to do this for about 20 minutes.)

Add the sharp shredded cheese slowly. Use a full 8-ounce bag—this is not the time to be cheesy. (Ha, get it, cheesy? lol) Once sauce is nice and thick, turn off the heat.

In a separate pan add water with salt and 1 teaspoon of olive oil and let boil.

Add large shells pasta and let cook for about 7 minutes or until al dente. Strain the water out but leave about ½ cup of pasta water in the pasta.

Place back on the stove on high heat. Add a small can of evaporated milk and butter and let melt. Add ½ of the cheese sauce. Let it simmer for about 2 minutes.

Get a baking pan. Place all cheese pasta inside the baking pan then cover with the remaining cheese sauce. Spread one 8 oz bag of extra sharp shredded cheese and sprinkle with black pepper.

Bake in the oven at 400 for about 10 minutes. Remove when top is golden and cheese and melted. Let sit for about 5 minutes, then enjoy.

Cat's Shrimp
(Peppered Shrimp)

I know you are probably saying, "Is this animal food. Why would I be cooking shrimp for a cat?" Very good questions but wait till you hear the answer to this madness. Who is Cat?

Cat is my daughter. Her actual name is Chantale. When she was a baby, my husband and I used to go to her room to give her a hug or a kiss and she would squirm and do these sounds that sounded like a cat. This kid has been weird since day one.

Oh, let me tell you about how she and I met. Three years after the birth of Nev, I gained an insane amount of weight and I was sick of it. I was fully committed to do something about it. I dedicated two hours a day, three days a week to go to the gym. I ate and slept right, drank a lot of water, and did everything right to lose the stubborn pounds. After six months, fully committed, I did it. I lost all the weight. I went from a size twelve to a size four. I was sexy, mama. I was getting head turns and I felt on top of the world. How can I blame my husband for resisting? I was his eye candy. The poor man couldn't wait to come home every night—and yup, you guessed it, I got pregnant. I gained all the weight back and gave birth to a nine-pound cat (Chantale). That's how we met. I have never been able to see a size four since her birth.

I take so much joy watching her grow. She is beautiful inside and out. She's smart, warm loving, and if she wasn't my daughter, she would be my best friend. She loves when I cook for her, and she loves this dish especially. I think it's because her and this dish share a lot in common: raw, hot and spicy, strong visual representation, and always underestimated. The result is explosive.

- 1 pound of shrimp with heads on
- 2 tablespoons butter
- 2 tablespoons olive oil
- 6 garlic cloves, crushed
- 1 tablespoon kosher salt
- 1 tablespoon garlic powder
- ½ one habanero pepper
- Juice of ½ one lemon

PREPARATION

In a hot pan, add olive oil and crushed garlic, then add ½ of one habanero pepper. Cover and let burn a little bit.

Add shrimp, salt, and garlic powder. Stir occasionally until spicy red. After 10 minutes add butter and some fresh lemon juice. Let simmer until juice is rendered. Enjoy.

Bougie Corn
(Baked Corn)

What is wrong with him? Sreiously. By him, I mean my husband, Jamal. Who says sh&$ like that? I have been married to this man for twenty four (24) years. We met when he was seventeen and I was twenty. I robbed the cradle. We were so young and knew nothing about life. I remember our first date was at this restaurant called El Torito on Route 4, Paramus, New Jersey. Our first meal was a chicken chimichanga and a chicken fajita. My favorite was the free tortilla chips they would put on the table while you wait for the food to arrive. Everything at El Torito had corn in it and man do I love corn. Maybe it's the little girl from Haiti in me who would be in the cornfield in the summer. I remembered picking a bunch of corn and going back and boiling them. That memory would never leave me. Jamal however, has a different relationship with corn. He just does not like corn. Do you know of anyone who does not like corn? Again, I ask, what is wrong with him? Here is my way of making corn. This should change your opinion of corn if you're not already a corn lover—go for it!

WHAT YOU WILL NEED

- Aluminum Foil – about a foot long
- Fresh corn
- A pat of butter
- A touch of kosher salt
- A touch of cracked black pepper
- A sprinkle of sugar

PREPARATION

Open the aluminum foil, peel the corn, place a pat of butter on top of the corn, then sprinkle a little salt, fresh cracked pepper, and a touch of sugar. Roll that baby up and bake at 350 degrees for 35 minutes. That's it. What's not to love?

This Uncivilized Chick!
(Baked Chicken Extraordinaire)

My first born, Genevievre Miller aka Nev—this chick has been a blessing since the second she was conceived. As a child, she was always strong minded and was a tough kid to mold. She knew what she wanted and when she wanted it and there wasn't anything anyone could do or say that would sway her otherwise. I am just fortunate the stubbornness was mostly positive. She was a lazy one. Nev would wait until the last minute to do any task and when she didn't want to do something, she would give you every pathetic reason to why she shouldn't. Her pathetic display was well thought out, and the way she presented it always seemed believable. She not only thinks wider, she thinks deeper. It was a raw talent she was born with. She was persuasive, sometimes you would wonder as an adult whether maybe she has a point—until you snapped back and realized nooooo, it's Nev being an artistic con and good at the craft of persuasion. Did I mention this was during her adolescent years!

The other side to her is that she is unequivocally a pure, gentle soul—the sweetest little girl you'll ever meet. However, when it comes to her dad and her sister – anyone who dares to do harm to them, Nev turns into this uncivilized chick that will surprise you. She and her father are extremely close. I always wonder when they are ever going to cut the umbilical cord between the two of them. She's also super protective of her baby sister and would kill for her. She believes she and only she has the right to abuse her sister; anyone else – look out she got daggers.

One of our favorite dishes to cook is this ginger wine chicken. It's a little complicated, but I promise you, this new experience is worth exploring and you will forever thank me.

WHAT YOU WILL NEED

- I whole rotisserie chicken or chicken quarters (If you are doing a whole chicken, cut the chicken from the front breast all the way down. Most people like to cut from the back and remove the neck and the ribs. Don't do that; that's discrimination if you ask me. Don't throw any of those pieces away—what did they do to you?)

- Juice of 1 squeezed lemon and 1 squeezed lime
- 1 tablespoon of Adobo seasoning
- 1 chicken bouillon cube
- 5 whole garlic cloves, crushed
- A handful of cilantro leaves mashed in a pilón
- 5 pieces of whole allspice, crushed
- 1 tablespoon cracked pepper
- 3 teaspoons tomato paste
- 1 tablespoon browning sauce
- 1 tablespoon soy sauce
- 1 tablespoon brown sugar
- 1 cup ginger wine
- 1 diced onion
- 2 tablespoons ketchup
- 2 tablespoons olive oil
- 1 tablespoon garlic powder
- 1 tablespoon onion powder
- 1/3 of one habanero pepper
- 2 sprigs of fresh thyme

PREPARATION

Wash chicken thoroughly with vinegar or lemon. Then pour the lemon/lime juice on top and add the crushed garlic, mashed cilantro, Adobo, chicken bouillon, smashed whole spice, cracked pepper, garlic powder, and onion powder. Let chicken marinated for at least 3 hours (overnight is even better).

When ready to bake, turn oven on at 350.

In one bowl, add ketchup, browning, soy sauce, brown sugar, olive oil, and ginger wine in one bowl. Mix vigorously.

Get baking bags. Add 2 tablespoons of flour and shake vigorously. Place chicken inside the bag. Add liquid content, thyme, and chopped onions.

Tie bag and bake in deep baking pan/dish at 350 for about 1 hour. Gently remove bag from pan, then add tomato paste. Let bake for another 30 minutes until golden.

Let sit for 15 minutes and enjoy.

Pierce United
(Tomato Cucumber Salad)

This is a story about a man name Ed Pierce. He played a huge role in my younger daughter's life in ways he will never know. He was president of my daughter's elementary school board and Ed is different in every way. He inspires others by being himself—just that simple. He never makes excuses for anything that seems difficult. When I am around him I always feel intimidated. He is so smart and always has big ideas. I just don't know of anyone who thinks that big about EVERYTHING.

Oh and get this, he expects you to think just as big as he does. He forces you to be a part of the community without you even realizing it. He demands the utmost best, and very often people misread his intentions. Instead, we thought (including myself) that he was being domineering, demanding, and egotistical. Man was I wrong! It was the opposite. You hear all the time when people say "I see the best in a person." No Ed, doesn't only see the best, he pulls out the best in every person and slams it on the table and says, "Here . . . you couldn't see this."

My daughter sized his character perfectly from the very beginning. She couldn't understand why he was being misjudged by everyone. She would say, "He just wants the best for everyone and everyone is just being too lazy to produce their best." She was right, and looking back now, Ed continues to be just an amazing human being.

Everyone knows what school plays are like. You attend because it's your kid on the stage, but as a parent when you watch this madness (you pray to baby Jesus) that your kid will have some other talent to present to the world. Ed has a theater background. He turned the school plays into first-class Broadway plays. I mean, they were so professionally done the first time my family and I saw one of the performances all I remembered us saying to each other when we got home was, "Wow. My god, that man brought greatness out of everyone who surrounds him." That's just Ed naturally.

Another example about his greatness: I remember having breakfast with Ed and another friend Kevin at a local town diner. Nothing fancy—it's a community restaurant where you always run into somebody you know. The food is not that great, but the atmosphere makes you feel cozy and comfortable.

Naturally I ordered waffle, Kevin ordered French toast, and here comes Ed. He found ways to create a plate that when it came out from the kitchen, even the waitress was shocked. It was egg whites with spinach and sliced tomatoes. The bread was toasted with just the right amount of color and the bacon was just the right amount, lined vertically side by side. The plate looked ready to be photographed. It was just the most beautiful plate of breakfast that I think the restaurant had ever produced.

This tomato salad is a little reflection of Ed Pierce. It's a combination of all types of tomatoes, and when done properly, the flavor is unexpected, with robust colors, and you will be forced to look at tomatoes differently.

WHAT YOU WILL NEED

- Tricolored cherry tomatoes or one beef tomato
- 1 cucumber
- Handful of parsley and cilantro leaves
- Handful of basil leaves
- 1 fresh rosemary leaf
- 2 tablespoons olive oil
- 2 tablespoons high-grade balsamic vinaigrette
- 1 teaspoon salt
- 1 tablespoon cracked pepper

PREPARATION

In one bowl, cut tomatoes in half. Add olive oil and balsamic vinaigrette.

Peel and cut cucumber into cubes.

Add salt, pepper, and chopped rosemary and fresh basil

Stir and enjoy.

Pick Your Balls
(Meatballs)
Ball 1: Turkey and Chicken | Ball 2:
Ground Pork, and Ground Beef

Stop judging me. Yes, my mind is in the gutter—so what? I live life to the fullest.

The first time I made this dish it was with red meat—ball 2. Then my younger daughter decided one day that she would no longer eat red meat and converted strictly to poultry. I grew up in southern Haiti. The Haitian culture is all about discipline, honor, and self-respect. Children barely get a say—you do what you're told and eat what's in front of you. There's no debate about what's for dinner. We didn't have Grubhub or Uber Eats and/or the likes. The idea of telling your parents you didn't like a meal was never even a thought, let alone deciding to not eat a select group of meat by choice. However, my American children challenge the Haitian in me all the time—and sad to say, they always win.

My poor husband loved ball 2, enjoyed it thoroughly, until one day it was all brought to a halt when my youngest daughter came home from school after a science class where they discussed about how red meat is bad for you. She wanted the entire house to change our diet and we had to convert to poultry entirely. He will tell you that he enjoys ball 1 just the same. However, if he had it his way he probably would choose ball 2.

WHAT YOU WILL NEED

- I chicken bouillon cube for ball I, but I beef bouillon cube for ball 2
- ½ lbs of ground chicken and ½ lbs of ground turkey (for BALL I.) OR
- ½ lbs of ground beef and ½ lbs of ground pork (for BALL 2)
- (The rest of the ingredients is universal for either)
- 2 eggs
- 2 slices white bread, soaked in milk
- A handful of parsley
- 2 sprigs of thyme

- 1 tablespoon black pepper
- 2 teaspoons Adobo
- ½ cup fresh diced tomatoes
- ½ cup chopped onions
- 5 fresh garlic cloves, crushed
- 1 tablespoon soy sauce
- Juice of ½ a lemon
- 5 pieces of whole allspice
- A sliver of habanero pepper
- 2 cups of all-purpose bleached flour

PREPARATION

Add all ingredients to a bowl and use your hands to mix them together. Let sit for about half an hour.

In a hot pan, add some vegetable oil and let it get to 400 degrees.

Place the flour on a plate. Use an ice cream scoop to measure the balls, big or small, depending on size of balls you want. Drop the balls into the flour. Roll with your hands until balls are fully coated.

Place each ball in the hot oil, keeping them half an inch away from each other. Let cook, then turn over to cook the other side.

When done, garnish and serve. Or, add tomato sauce and let it render for about 10 minutes on medium heat then serve with my Laisser-Faire Mashed Potatoes on the next page.

Laisser-Faire Mashed Potatoes (Double-Mashed Potatoes)

This dish is a perfect representation of my husband's personality. His name is Jamal, but I call him J. He is often the calm one in any situation. He has always seemed passive, calculated, and dormant, and shows minimal aggression. What attracted me to J is how smart he is. He speaks with clarity and determination. He has been working in the retail space for over twenty years. At one point he was running about fourteen stores for a very popular sporting goods store. They always counted on him to get the job done, but being who he is, didn't need any motivation or approval from anyone to acknowledge his efforts. In his mind it's about committing to what he promised. His word is his bond.

The flip side of that is I've witnessed people taking advantage of him—and I mean everyone, from his own family members to all those he reports to. I always thought he would change. Maybe one day he will be a little more like me—a little more aggressive and tell people to back off. That's not him; that's not in his DNA.

This mashed potato dish is probably one of my favorite things to cook for him. It's simple, and just when you think it's done, there's the last step that makes it stand out—Enjoy!

WHAT YOU WILL NEED

- 7 or 8 golden potatoes
- 5 or 6 garlic cloves
- 1 tablespoon olive oil
- 2 tablespoons kosher salt
- 1 tablespoon cracked black pepper
- 3 teaspoons salted butter
- 1 8-oz can of evaporated milk
- ½ cup grated parmesan cheese
- 1 tablespoon sour cream

Place garlic cloves in aluminum foil. Add olive oil, a little kosher salt, and cracked black pepper. Fold and bake on 350 degrees for about 20 minutes.

Cut the potatoes in half. Wash thoroughly and boil with salt water for about 15 minutes.

Empty boiled water and rinse potatoes with cold water.

Gently scooped the potatoes from their skin and place in a bowl. The skins should have a little firmness to them with some of the potatoes still left inside.

Take all the skins and lay them in baking pan spread about 5 inches apart from each other. Add a touch of butter at the bottom of each potato skin

Take the potato in the bowl and add the roasted garlic cloves and butter. Mash rigorously until the consistency is soft and smooth. Add evaporated milk and mix with a spatula. Then add parmesan cheese, cracked black pepper, and sour cream. Mix thoroughly.

Take a scoop or two of the mashed potatoes and place in each potato skin. When done, sprinkle a little more parmesan cheese on top and a little more cracked black pepper.

Place in the oven at 400 degrees for about 10 minutes until lightly baked. You think you're done, not quite. There's one more thing . . .

Turn the oven to broil under low and let broil for about 90 seconds. Take out and serve. They're absolutely out of this world delicious.

Radical Hawaiian Chick
(Chicken Sandwich)

My daughter Cat went to Hawaii with her best friend Kelsey to celebrate Kelsey's sweet sixteen. Yes, you heard me right—parents have taken sweet sixteen to a whole new level. I remembered being fortunate when someone used to call me on the landline on the day of my birthday. I was so grateful, and I knew I had the responsibility to return the favor on their birthday. Those were the days when kindness and thoughtfulness meant something. How did we go from that to backyard birthday parties, then renting a hall, then booking a weekend getaway, to now long-distance traveling? What have we done to our kids?

(Oh yes, I did the same thing by sending my kids to South Africa to celebrate her 16th birthday. So, I too live in a glass house, I have no business throwing stones.)

This dish is to honor this amazing trip she experienced in Hawaii and how radical the world has become.

WHAT YOU WILL NEED

- Chicken breast, sliced thin
- A couple slices pineapple
- 2 tablespoons olive oil
- 1 fresh rosemary sprig
- 1 tablespoon kosher salt
- 1 tablespoon cracked pepper
- Romaine Lettuce
- Sliced beef tomatoes
- 1 tablespoon BBQ sauce
- Potato bread
- The juice of one lemon
- 1 teaspoon honey
- ½ teaspoon of Mayonnaise
- Sliced red onions

PREPARATION

In a bowl, add olive oil, rosemary, salt, cracked pepper, honey, and lemon juice. Place chicken inside and let it marinate overnight. Next day, place chicken on the grill. Keep brushing chicken with the marinade so the chicken remains moist. When fully cooked, remove and let it rest. Add pineapple on grill and keep brushing with the marinate for about 5 minutes

LET'S BUILD

Get a potato roll. Swipe the top bun with a little mayo, add red onions, add about a teaspoon of BBQ sauce, then add lettuce, and tomato.

Place the cooked chicken and pineapple on the bottom bun. Merge them together, cut in half, then enjoy.

What a Jerk!
(Jerk Chicken)

When the girls were young my husband used to work on average sixty-five hours per week. He worked as a general manager in retail stores. His position was always demanding. In exchange, we had limited family time so the times we spent together were sacred. For the most part, I felt like a single mother and the way I dealt with the loneliness was making sure the girls were always busy. I signed them up for competitive cheer, which required them to be at practice at least three to four days a week, Kumon two times a week, private tumbling once a week, and God knows what other activities were included in their schedule.

The girls didn't feel his absence as much because they were so busy. I kept a very militant home and their schooling was first and foremost. On days when all of us were together, we would do family night. Family night was always fun. It was a must that I prepared every one's favorite and did a buffet spread. The girls would pick a movie and we would put the surround sound on like we were in a movie theater and just chill. We would eat as much or as little we chose—no judgement from anyone.

Looking back now, I think this was the best tradition we could have instilled in our family. To this day, we still do family night and it allows us to be us.

One of our favorite dishes is jerk chicken. Sometimes, I would get the premade jerk sauce from the store when I wanted to be lazy. However, on most days I like my jerk sauce from scratch. Here we go.

WHAT YOU WILL NEED

- 2 lbs of Chicken wings
- 4 sprigs of Fresh thyme
- 5 scallion stems
- A handful of cilantro
- 3 tablespoons olive oil
- 2 tablespoons kosher salt
- 2 tablespoons cracked black pepper
- 1 whole habanero pepper
- One peeled onion
- ½ cup chopped ginger
- 3 tablespoons soy sauce
- 5 roasted garlic cloves
- 1 tablespoon cinnamon
- 1 tablespoon unbleached flour
- 1 teaspoon nutmeg
- 1 cup apple cider vinegar
- 1 cup white vinegar
- ½ cup brown sugar
- 1 tablespoon crushed allspice

PREPARATION

Place the wings in a large bowl and add about 1 cup of white vinegar. Rinse the wings and wash thoroughly with water.

In a blender, take the rest of the ingredients listed above and blend them together. Add about 3 Tablespoon of the mixture to the wings. Place seasoned wings and add 1 teaspoon of flour inside the baking pan. Cover and bake at 350 degrees for about 45 minutes. Remove cover and bring up the heat to 385 degrees. Continue to bake for another 15 minutes until golden brown. Let sit for 5 minutes and enjoy.

Gena Summer's Garden (Chicken Salad)

I relish the times I spend with my girls. They are not just a part of my life, they are my life. I make it a point to coexist with them, to breathe their air, to be their voice, to finish their sentences, and to be a part of their mental well-being. I invited them into my life. While many would say, "My kids should be the one that's grateful that I gave them life," it's the opposite for me. They gave me life. They entered my world when I asked them to. They have provided me unconditional love and that's a gift that I will never take for granted. It's the purest love one can experience.

Their friends enjoy coming to the house because I provide a safe space for them to just be, to be kids. I used this time, to really listen, to provide guidance and let them know that adults are people too. When presented with a good meal, you get to hear all the Tea, the real Tea, not the tea they tell their parents. I have learned just as much from them as they have probably learned from me

This salad became famous through no fault of my daughter's, as she was just eating a bowl of salad during her lunch period at school. Next thing she knew, she was surrounded by her friends. One by one, they were picking some of the ingredients and before she knew it, half of her salad was gone. The solution—there would be salad Mondays. Cat would pick five of her friends and she would bring salads for them.

The word got around to the parents and the school administration acknowledged I make the best chicken salad. When I arrived to any school functions or ran into anyone in administration, the first question I would get asked before exchanging pleasantries would be, "What's so damn special about this chicken salad that I hear about?"

Here's the blueprint for how to create this piece of heaven. Have fun with it.

(measurement is totally up to you – you're the boss on this one)

For the salad
- Shredded cabbage
- Chopped romaine lettuce
- Lemon juice
- Chopped figs
- Cherry tomatoes/ kumato tomatoes/ plum tomatoes, cut in in half or bite-size
- Jalapeno peppers sliced very thin
- Red grapes and green grapes, cut in half
- Tangerine, cut in chunk sizes
- Sliced apples, green and Macintosh
- Brown sugar roasted walnuts
- Green peppers and red peppers
- Blueberries and raspberries
- Strawberries sliced laser thin
- Blue cheese or mozzarella cheese

For the dressing
- ½ cup of Olive oil
- A handful of Cilantro
- 1 each of fresh squeezed Lime and lemon juice
- 1 teaspoon of Salt
- 1 teaspoon of Black pepper
- 8-10 pieces of Blueberries or raspberries
- A sliver of jalapeno
- 1 tablespoon of honey

PREPARATION

In a large bowl combine all salad ingredients. Toss it all up.

In a blender, add dressing ingredients and blend. Toss dressing into salad.

Add grilled chicken and you will have a party whether it was intended or not.

Walls of love
(Yuca)

Her name is Iris Walls. She fills my cup and she is the center of my village. Her daughter, Gabriella is my daughter's best friend. They have been friends since Kindergarten. Iris and I have had our share of conversations about the girls. There were days when we had no clue what we were doing as parents, and our conversations would sound like the blind leading the blind.

One morning Iris texted me a picture of what Gabriella had decided to wear to school. She and Gabby were going through a screaming match and Gabriella was in full fledge teenage mode. It was a war between two strong minded women, the estrogen in the house was high and it was one of those mornings that can bleed through the rest of your day. I called Iris and told her to go to work and leave Gabriella at home and that I would take her to school. She thanked me both for being a friend and for saving Gabriella's life because she was going to kill her. I laughed and hang up the phone. Twenty minutes later, I arrived at the house and texted Gabriella to come down to my car. Since Iris had already told her that I was on my way, she had quickly changed her clothes to something more appropriate for school. She hoped in my car, smiles and all - as if it were an ordinary morning and nothing had happened.

Since I am not skilled enough to understand the psycho mental state of teenagers, when Gabriella got in the car, I smiled back turned the music up and started driving. Before I dropped her to school, I took her to a nearby coffee shop for an ice drink, gave her a small pep talk and asked her to stop driving her mother crazy. She agreed, gave me a hug, and went off to school.

One thing I know with a 100% certainty, they both love each other to pieces. I call it Walls of love.

Looking back now it was not funny at the time, but man it is hilarious now.

This dish is to memorialize our memories for all the moms who played a part in my village and allowed me to be a part of theirs.

- ½ a Yuka, peeled and cut into cubes
- 2 cloves of garlic
- 1 chopped red onion

PREPARATION

In a small pan, cover with water and 1 tablespoon of salt.

Let boil for 7 minutes. Drain water when done.

In a saucepan,

¼ cup of olive oil, 2 cloves of garlic cloves (semi crushed), 1 red onions (sliced)

Let onions and garlic get fully caramelized, then add yuca. Let simmer for about 3 minutes and transfer to a plate. Enjoy.

To my girls—Genevievre a.k.a Nev, and Chantale a.k.a Cat—the reason I live and breathe every day. Thank you for accepting the invitation to the party that I call my life. I must have done something right in my previous life to be rewarded with your presences. All the weight I gained while pregnant with you both, and all the labor pain, was so worth it. Would I do it again?
ABSOFREAKINLUTELY.

Critics......

"Auntie Gena's recipes are the secret family recipes we all wish we knew, complete with the funny stories behind them. They are all packed with flavor that will elevate your next Sunday dinner, and that's a promise!"
—Melissa Agaba

"With flavors as varied and genuine as the life stories conveyed within, *Gena's Pots and Pans* is an ideal introduction to homestyle island cooking. We loved these recipes! The medley of dishes are dinner party worthy, while remaining accessible enough for a casual date night. *Un délice*!
—Amal and Jonathan Fung

Full of passion and emotion, this is the woman who I have come to know these many years and it is this that she puts into each and every dish.
—Jamal Miller

Co-author
Genevievre Miller

Born and raised in Teaneck New Jersey, Genevievre earned a double degree in Political Science and African studies at Pennsylvania State University. This book was created with her single idea of putting all the recipes together as a legacy for the family. She loves learning about new cultures, new dishes, and new recipes. Her goal is to one day be a Congresswoman and practice law in the public sector.

Author's Biography:
Gena Miller

Born in Haiti then immigrating to America at a young age, Gena has been able to blend the two cultures into a culinary experience that is both familiar and uniquely her own. As you explore this book you will not only enjoy the tastes but go on a journey of her life experiences and stories that will bring her world closer to yours. Jwi manje ou ("Enjoy your meal" -in Creole)

In Memoriam of
Jude Yves Silien
May 13, 1968 - August 5, 2020

CPSIA information can be obtained
at www.ICGtesting.com
Printed in the USA
LVHW070133230920
666820LV00009B/502